Langenscheidt

And pigs might fly

**Bildhaft sprechen mit
250 englischen Redewendungen**

von Dr. Helen Galloway

Langenscheidt

München · Wien

Bildnachweis:
Shutterstock: Jiri Hera – S. 6; Lana Langlois – S. 7; Oksana Kuzmina – S. 7; Cat'chy
Images – S. 7; Joe Gough – S. 18; neil langan – S. 18; kb-photodesign – S. 30;
SvetaZi – S. 42; Viorel Sima – S. 54; Happy monkey – S. 55; Leena Robinson – S. 66;
Le Do – S. 79; Oleg Mikhaylov – S. 90; Super Prin – S. 102/103; martin951 – S. 114;
Somchai Som – S. 128

And pigs might fly
Herausgegeben von der Langenscheidt-Redaktion

Projektleitung: Julia Zweigle
Autorin: Dr. Helen Galloway
Lektor: Dr. Lutz Walther
Layout: Volk Agentur + Verlag
Illustrationen Cover und Innenteil: Daniela Grabner
Corporate Design Umschlag: KW43 BRANDDESIGN, Düsseldorf

www.langenscheidt.com

© 2018 Langenscheidt GmbH & Co. KG, München
Satz: Volk Agentur + Verlag, München
Druck und Bindung: Druckerei C. H. Beck, Nördlingen

ISBN 978-3-468-43125-8

18010

Vorwort

Sie unterhalten sich mit Freunden auf Englisch, aber leider verstehen Sie nicht, um was es im Gespräch geht. Um Ihre Freunde darauf hinzuweisen, sagen Sie einfach: *„I'm sorry. I only understand railway station!"* Ihre Freunde sehen Sie verständnislos an, denn jetzt sind sie es, die *„nur Bahnhof verstehen"*.

An diesem Beispiel sieht man, dass es oft nicht ausreicht, nur die Vokabeln und Grammatikregeln einer Fremdsprache zu beherrschen. Gerade die bildhafte Sprache ist in der Alltagssprache allgegenwärtig. Manchmal können diese sogenannten idiomatischen Wendungen und Ausdrücke aus der Muttersprache wortwörtlich in die Fremdsprache übersetzt werden. Zum Beispiel sagt auch ein Englischsprechender, dass er grün vor Neid wird: *„I'm green with envy."* Dass eine wortwörtliche Übersetzung funktioniert, ist jedoch eher selten der Fall.

Bildhafte Ausdrücke sind meist kulturell geprägt, weshalb in Fremdsprachen oft andere Bilder verwendet werden als sie für den deutschen Muttersprachler üblich sind. Möchten Sie auf Englisch sagen, dass Ihnen ein Raum zu klein ist? Kein Problem: *„There's no room to swing a cat."* Katzenschwingen? Das ist für den Deutschsprachigen ein recht ungewöhnliches Bild, für den Englischsprachigen jedoch sehr gebräuchlich.

Dieses Buch dient als Einführung in die wunderbare Welt der englischen Redewendungen. Insgesamt werden 252 der gebräuchlichsten englischen Wendungen aufgeführt, die in neun Themengebiete unterteilt sind. Jede Redewendung wird wortwörtlich und idiomatisch ins Deutsche übersetzt. So verstehen Sie zum einen das Bild, das im Englischen verwendet wird, und zum anderen erfahren Sie, wie Sie den Ausdruck am besten ins Deutsche übersetzen können. Außerdem zeigt ein englischer Beispielsatz, wie die Redewendung in der Alltagssprache verwendet wird. Bei sehr *umgangssprachlichen Ausdrücken* warnt ein Icon (ugs.) vor einer unpassenden Verwendung. Zur Auflockerung wird in jedem Kapitel eine Redewendung illustriert. Zusätzlich gibt es zu allen Themengebieten eine *Quizfrage* sowie Infofenster über *Falsche Freunde* und *Fettnäpfchen* bzw. *lustige Missverständnisse*, die durch falsche Verwendung und / oder Übersetzung entstehen können. Ein kleiner Test rundet jedes Kapitel ab. Die Lösungen dazu sowie zwei Register in beide Sprachrichtungen, in denen alle Redewendungen nach dem jeweiligen Schlagwort sortiert sind, finden Sie am Ende des Buches.

Viel Spaß bei Ihrem Einstieg in die Welt der englischen Redewendungen!

„It's the greatest thing since sliced bread!"

Inhaltsverzeichnis

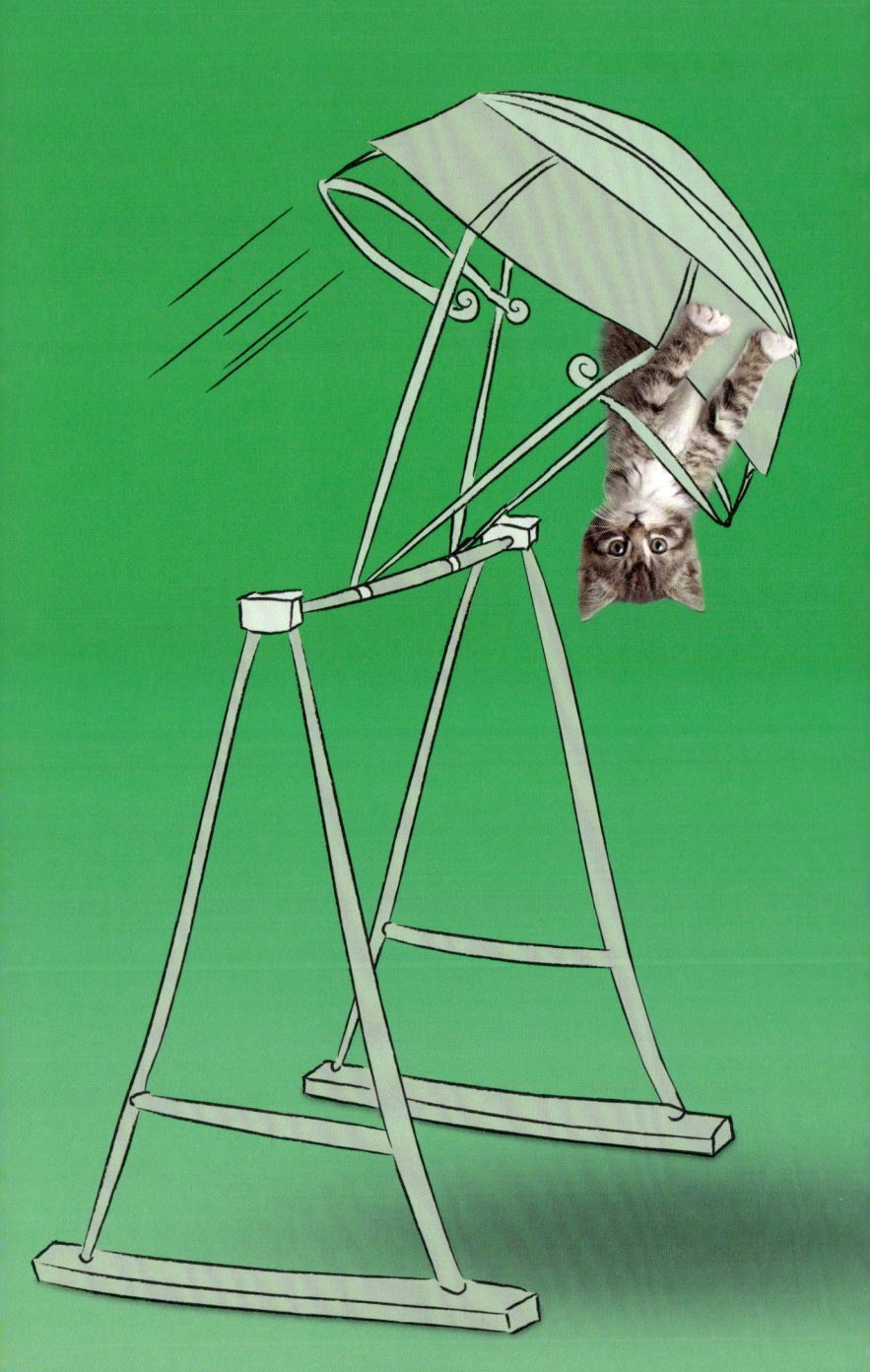

Tierisch gut!

there's no room to swing a cat
es gibt kaum Platz sich umzudrehen

to be as blind as a bat
wörtlich: blind wie eine Fledermaus sein
idiomatisch: blind wie ein Maulwurf sein

Where did I leave my glasses?
I'm as blind as a bat without them.

to be like a bear with a sore head
wörtlich: wie ein Bär mit Kopfschmerzen sein
idiomatisch: ein richtiger Brummbär sein

Don't disturb your father. You know he's like a bear
with a sore head on Sunday mornings.

 to think you are the bee's knees
wörtlich: sich für die Knie der Biene halten
idiomatisch: sich für den Größten halten

George thinks he's the bee's knees with his new sports car.

to kill two birds with one stone
wörtlich: zwei Vögel mit einem Stein töten
idiomatisch: zwei Fliegen mit einer Klappe schlagen

Let's kill two birds with one stone and go to the DIY store
on the way to the bank.

to be like a bull in a china shop

wörtlich: wie ein Stier im Porzellanladen sein

idiomatisch: wie ein Elefant im Porzellanladen sein

These negotiations are very delicate.
We can't send James. He's like a bull in a china shop
and will ruin everything.

to have butterflies in your stomach

wörtlich: Schmetterlinge im Magen / Bauch haben

idiomatisch: ein flaues Gefühl in der Magengegend haben

Tom woke up with butterflies in his stomach.
He was going for that big job interview today.

Verliebtheit oder Übelkeit?

„Schmetterlinge im Bauch haben" ist im Deutschen sehr gebräuchlich – allerdings heißt es bei uns Glücksgefühle haben oder verliebt sein. Der englische Gebrauch drückt aus, dass man nervös ist, aber aus verschiedenen Gründen. Wenn man also hört *„I had butterflies in my stomach before going to the dentist",* hat das sicherlich nichts mit der Liebe zum Zahnarzt zu tun!

to grin like a Cheshire cat

wörtlich: grinsen wie eine Katze aus Cheshire

idiomatisch: grinsen wie ein Honigkuchenpferd

Beth heard that she'd won a million pounds on the lottery and she's been grinning like a Cheshire cat ever since.

to let the cat out of the bag

wörtlich: die Katze aus der Tasche lassen

idiomatisch: die Katze aus dem Sack lassen

The party was meant to be a big surprise, but then your mum let the cat out of the bag when she asked you if she should bring a cake.

to put the cat among the pigeons

wörtlich: die Katze unter die Tauben bringen

idiomatisch: für Aufregung sorgen; Unruhe stiften

The boss's girlfriend has been promoted to manager instead of Steve? That's going to put the cat among the pigeons.

there's no room to swing a cat

wörtlich: es gibt keinen Platz, um eine Katze hin- und herzuschwingen

idiomatisch: es gibt kaum Platz sich umzudrehen

The flat was in a great location but it was tiny. There was no room to swing a cat in the kitchen.

 to be chicken

wörtlich: Huhn sein

idiomatisch: ein Angsthase sein

That spider is tiny. Don't be chicken.
Go and catch it and put it outside.

you can't teach an old dog new tricks

wörtlich: man kann einem alten Hund keine neuen
  Kunststücke beibringen

idiomatisch: der Mensch ist ein Gewohnheitstier;
  was Hänschen nicht lernt, lernt Hans nimmermehr

I've tried teaching my grandad how to use the Internet,
but it's hopeless. You can't teach an old dog new tricks.

Alles klar?

Hört man den Satz „*don't be chicken*",
handelt es sich um …

a) *ein Lob.*
b) *einen Hilferuf.*
c) *einen Vorwurf.*

to be able to talk the hind leg off a donkey

wörtlich: einem Esel das Hinterbein abreden können

idiomatisch: jemandem die Ohren abkauen

I had to sit next to the president and listen to his golfing stories the whole evening. That man can talk the hind leg off a donkey!

to take to something like a duck to water

wörtlich: sich zu etwas hingezogen fühlen, wie eine Ente zum Wasser

idiomatisch: bei etwas sofort in seinem Element sein

Matthew has taken to karate like a duck to water. He can already break a piece of wood in two with his bare hands!

to feel like a fish out of water

wörtlich: sich wie ein Fisch aus dem Wasser fühlen

idiomatisch: sich wie ein Fisch auf dem Trockenen fühlen

Becca felt like a fish out of water at her new school. All the other pupils came from a different town.

to be the only fly in the ointment

wörtlich: die einzige Fliege in der Salbe sein

idiomatisch: das einzige Haar in der Suppe sein (auch: der einzige Haken an der Sache sein)

The boss liked her project proposal, but the only fly in the ointment was that there was no money to fund it.

(s)he wouldn't hurt a fly

wörtlich: er / sie würde keiner Fliege etwas zuleide tun

idiomatisch: er / sie kann keiner Fliege etwas zuleide tun

It couldn't have been Tim who sent those horrible emails to Gaby. He wouldn't hurt a fly.

to get somebody's goat

wörtlich: jemandes Ziege kriegen

idiomatisch: jemanden auf die Palme bringen

Whenever the prime minister appears on TV, my dad turns it off. She just gets his goat.

– to get somebody's goat –

13

to go the whole hog

wörtlich: das ganze Mastschwein gehen

idiomatisch: aufs Ganze gehen

Joe and Gemma decided to go the whole hog and order a new suite instead of just an armchair.

to be straight from the horse's mouth

wörtlich: direkt aus dem Pferdemaul sein

idiomatisch: aus erster Quelle / Hand sein

"I don't believe Sharon said I was lazy."
"Well, go and ask Graham. He heard it straight from the horse's mouth."

I could eat a horse

wörtlich: ich könnte ein Pferd essen

idiomatisch: ich habe einen Bärenhunger

Are you coming for lunch? I missed breakfast this morning, so now I could eat a horse!

to get the lion's share

wörtlich: den Löwenanteil bekommen

idiomatisch: den Löwenanteil bekommen

The Labour Party did reasonably well in the election, but it was the Conservatives who got the lion's share of the vote.

and pigs might fly

wörtlich: und Schweine könnten fliegen

idiomatisch: wer's glaubt, wird selig

"Well, perhaps we'll get a pay rise next year."
"Yes, and pigs might fly."

 ## to pig yourself

wörtlich: sich schweinen

idiomatisch: sich vollstopfen

Ooh, my stomach hurts!
I shouldn't have pigged myself at the free buffet.

Kuriose Essgewohnheiten

Die englische Redewendung „*I could eat a horse*" hört man sehr oft. Als Nichtmuttersprachler muss man sie aber mit etwas Vorsicht verwenden. Es kann sein, dass die anderen Tischgäste es wörtlich nehmen, wenn sie die Essgewohnheiten der Deutschen nicht kennen und Angst um ihre Pferde und Ponys bekommen!

to rule the roost
wörtlich: den Schlafplatz / Hühnerstall regieren
idiomatisch: Herr im Haus sein; die Hosen anhaben

At work it was Sam who was in charge,
but at home it was his wife who ruled the roost.

to separate the sheep from the goats
wörtlich: die Schafe von den Ziegen trennen
idiomatisch: die Schafe von den Böcken trennen

The interviewers had created a more difficult test
to try to separate the sheep from the goats.

to have a whale of a time
wörtlich: einen Wal von einer Zeit haben
idiomatisch: einen Mordsspaß haben;
  sich königlich amüsieren

That new amusement park is just brilliant.
The kids had a whale of a time.

to keep the wolf from the door
wörtlich: den Wolf von der Tür fernhalten
idiomatisch: den größten Hunger stillen

Gary's job as a cleaner doesn't pay much,
but it's enough to keep the wolf from the door.

Alles verstanden?

Welche Redewendung passt zu welcher deutschen Entsprechung? Tragen Sie den Buchstaben der passenden Übersetzung in das Kästchen ein.

1. ☐ *to have a whale of a time*

2. ☐ *to be as blind as a bat*

3. ☐ *to think you are the bee's knees*

4. ☐ *to get somebody's goat*

5. ☐ *to pig yourself*

6. ☐ *to grin like a Cheshire cat*

7. ☐ *to kill two birds with one stone*

8. ☐ *to go the whole hog*

9. ☐ *to be chicken*

10. ☐ *you can't teach an old dog new tricks*

a. ein Angsthase sein **b.** grinsen wie ein Honigkuchenpferd
c. aufs Ganze gehen **d.** einen Mordsspaß haben
e. der Mensch ist ein Gewohnheitstier **f.** sich vollstopfen
g. blind wie ein Maulwurf sein **h.** sich für den Größten halten
i. zwei Fliegen mit einer Klappe schlagen **j.** jemanden auf die Palme bringen

Kapitel 2

Gefundenes Fressen

to be just pie in the sky
nur Luftschlösser sein

to bring home the bacon
wörtlich: den Speck nach Hause bringen
idiomatisch: die Brötchen verdienen

Brian and Marie decided that he would give up his job and become a house husband while she continued to bring home the bacon.

 ## to go bananas
wörtlich: Bananen gehen
idiomatisch: ausflippen; ausrasten

When Mum saw the state of the house after the party, she went bananas.

 ## to be full of beans
wörtlich: voller Bohnen sein
idiomatisch: putzmunter sein; völlig aufgekratzt sein

The dog is full of beans this morning. Look at him chasing that squirrel!

 ## to spill the beans
wörtlich: die Bohnen verschütten
idiomatisch: etwas verraten; etwas ausplaudern

The police were waiting at the bank for the robbers, so somebody must have spilled the beans.

 to take the biscuit

wörtlich: den Keks nehmen

idiomatisch: echt der Hammer sein; den Vogel abschießen

The price of tickets is going up and now they're going to reduce the number of trains? That just takes the biscuit.

 to be the greatest thing since sliced bread

wörtlich: das Größte seit Schnittbrot sein

idiomatisch: das Größte seit der Erfindung der Bratkartoffel sein

My sister thinks her e-book reader is the greatest thing since sliced bread, but I prefer to read a real book with pages in it.

Nicht alle Kekse sind süß

Mit der Redewendung „*that takes the biscuit*" drückt man Ärger und / oder Überraschung aus. Aber das sagt man nur in Großbritannien. In den USA sagt man „*that takes the cake*". Übrigens: „*biscuit*" bedeutet im Amerikanischen ohnehin etwas anderes. Es ist kein Plätzchen wie in Großbritannien, sondern ein kleines weiches Brötchen, das man mit Fleischsoße oder Marmelade isst.

to know which side your bread is buttered on

wörtlich: wissen, auf welcher Seite dein Brot mit Butter bestrichen ist

idiomatisch: wissen, wo etwas zu holen ist

Andy is always telling his mother-in-law how lovely she looks. He knows which side his bread is buttered on.

 ## to have a bun in the oven

wörtlich: ein süßes Teilchen im Backofen haben

idiomatisch: einen Braten in der Röhre haben

Nina has only been going out with Tom for three months and she's already got a bun in the oven.

 ## to butter somebody up

wörtlich: jemanden einbuttern

idiomatisch: jemandem Honig ums Maul schmieren

I tried buttering my neighbour up by admiring his roses, but he still wouldn't let me borrow his lawnmower.

 ## to be a piece of cake

wörtlich: ein Stück Kuchen sein

idiomatisch: ein Kinderspiel sein

"Did you have any problems finding your way around on the Tube in London?" "Not at all. It was a piece of cake really."

to be the icing on the cake
wörtlich: der Zuckerguss auf dem Kuchen sein
idiomatisch: das Tüpfelchen auf dem i sein

Sam had loved the concert. And getting the lead singer's autograph had just been the icing on the cake.

to sell like hot cakes
wörtlich: wie warme Kuchen verkaufen
idiomatisch: wie warme Semmeln weggehen

Since that supermodel was seen carrying one of these handbags, they've been selling like hot cakes.

Alles klar?

Hört man den Satz „*that exam was a piece of cake*", dann ist damit gemeint:

a) *Man hat gerade eine Backprüfung abgelegt.*
b) *Man ist sicher, dass man die Prüfung nicht bestanden hat.*
c) *Man fand die Prüfung sehr einfach.*

 to be a big cheese

wörtlich: ein großer Käse sein

idiomatisch: ein hohes Tier sein

Katie's dad may be able to help.
He's some kind of big cheese on the local council.

to be like chalk and cheese

wörtlich: wie Kreide und Käse sein

idiomatisch: wie Tag und Nacht sein

"Do you get on well with your sister?"
"Not really. We look similar, but as personalities
we're like chalk and cheese."

 that's the way the cookie crumbles

wörtlich: so zerkrümelt der Keks

idiomatisch: so läuft der Hase; so ist das Leben

It seems unfair that our best young players are bought by
the richer clubs, but that's the way the cookie crumbles.

to eat your words

wörtlich: deine Wörter essen

idiomatisch: Gesagtes zurücknehmen

The trainer says I'll never get in the football team,
but I'm going to make him eat his words.

to put all your eggs in one basket
wörtlich: alle deine Eier in einen Korb legen
idiomatisch: alles auf eine Karte / ein Pferd setzen

Fiona applied to study at Oxford University, but as she didn't want to put all her eggs in one basket, she applied to Edinburgh and Bristol as well.

to be a tough nut to crack
wörtlich: eine harte Nuss zu knacken sein
idiomatisch: eine harte Nuss sein; ein harter Brocken sein

The first two questions on the exam paper were easy, but the third one was a tough nut to crack.

– to be a big cheese –

 to do your nut

wörtlich: deine Nuss tun

idiomatisch: durchdrehen

My mum's going to do her nut when she hears how much I've spent on clothes this weekend.

in a nutshell

wörtlich: in einer Nussschale

idiomatisch: kurz gesagt; mit einem Wort

The company's sales have been very bad and they spent a lot of money trying to get into the Chinese market. In a nutshell, they've gone bankrupt.

 to go pear-shaped

wörtlich: birnenförmig werden

idiomatisch: schiefgehen; völlig danebengehen

Sue had organized everything carefully, but when the removal van didn't turn up, all her plans went pear-shaped.

 to be as easy as pie

wörtlich: so einfach wie Pastete sein

idiomatisch: kinderleicht sein

I find sudoku really difficult, but my brother says they're as easy as pie.

 to be just pie in the sky
wörtlich: nur Pastete im Himmel sein
idiomatisch: alles nur Luftschlösser sein;
  leere Versprechungen sein

Ian and Tess have been talking about opening a
restaurant, but I don't think they can afford it.
I think it's just pie in the sky.

 to be a hot potato
wörtlich: eine heiße Kartoffel sein
idiomatisch: ein heißes Eisen sein

The prime minister avoided talking about gay marriage
because it was such a political hot potato.

Mathe-Laien aufgepasst!

Wenn jemand mit der Redewendung *„to be as easy as pie"*
nicht so gut vertraut ist, kann es sein, dass er glaubt, jemand
prahle mit seinem mathematischen Können. Denn im Englischen spricht man *„pie"* genauso aus wie *„pi"*, die Zahl Pi.
„So einfach wie die Zahl Pi" – das sagt wohl nur ein zweiter
Einstein. Vielleicht ist das also eigentlich gar kein falscher
Freund, sondern ein guter?

to take something with a pinch of salt

wörtlich: etwas mit einer Prise Salz nehmen

idiomatisch: etwas nicht für bare Münze nehmen;
etwas mit Vorsicht genießen

The boss is always coming up with crazy ideas.
You have to take what she says with a pinch of salt.

 ## to be one sandwich short of a picnic

wörtlich: um ein Sandwich ein Picknick verfehlen

idiomatisch: nicht alle Tassen im Schrank haben;
nicht der / die Hellste sein

Whoever decided to organize the conference on
24th December was one sandwich short of a picnic.

 ## to get in a stew about something

wörtlich: über etwas in einen Eintopf geraten

idiomatisch: sich über etwas aufregen

Elizabeth could only have 50 guests at her wedding and
got into a real stew about who to invite.

not to be your cup of tea

wörtlich: nicht deine Tasse Tee sein

idiomatisch: nicht jemandes Fall sein

Visiting museums really isn't his cup of tea.
He'd much rather go and watch a rugby match.

Alles verstanden?

Welche Redewendung passt zu welcher deutschen Entsprechung? Tragen Sie den Buchstaben der passenden Übersetzung in das Kästchen ein.

1. ☐ *to butter somebody up*
2. ☐ *to spill the beans*
3. ☐ *to take something with a pinch of salt*
4. ☐ *to be one sandwich short of a picnic*
5. ☐ *to sell like hot cakes*
6. ☐ *to go pear-shaped*
7. ☐ *to have a bun in the oven*
8. ☐ *in a nutshell*
9. ☐ *to bring home the bacon*
10. ☐ *to go bananas*

a. die Brötchen verdienen **b.** einen Braten in der Röhre haben **c.** nicht alle Tassen im Schrank haben
d. etwas verraten **e.** ausflippen **f.** etwas nicht für bare Münze nehmen **g.** kurz gesagt **h.** völlig danebengehen
i. wie warme Semmeln weggehen **j.** jemandem Honig ums Maul schmieren

Reine Kopfsache

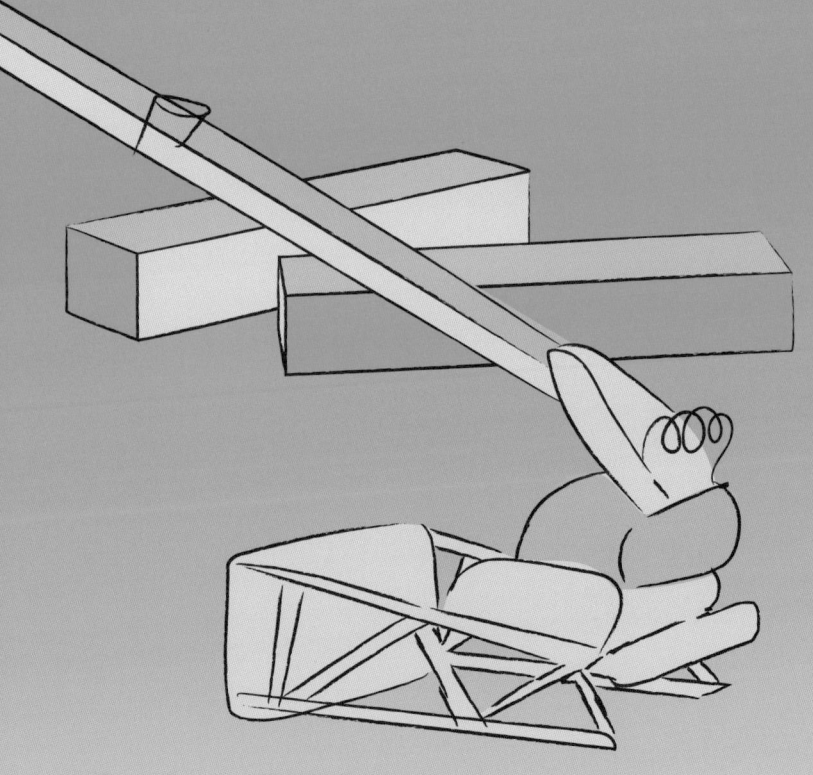

to bend somebody's ear
jemanden volltexten

to keep your chin up

wörtlich: dein Kinn hochhalten

idiomatisch: die Ohren steifhalten; Kopf hoch!

Keep your chin up! It's only three weeks until we get paid.

to be all ears

wörtlich: alle Ohren sein

idiomatisch: ganz Ohr sein

"Did I tell you that Martin's got a new girlfriend?"
"No, tell me all about her. I'm all ears."

 ### to bend somebody's ear

wörtlich: jemandem das Ohr biegen

idiomatisch: jemanden volltexten

Mike spent the whole evening bending my ear about his DVD collection.

 ### to go in one ear and out the other

wörtlich: zum einen Ohr herein- und zum anderen hinausgehen

idiomatisch: zum einen Ohr herein- und zum anderen hinausgehen

My daughter has explained texting to me twenty times, but it just seems to go in one ear and out the other.

to play it by ear

wörtlich: es nach dem Ohr spielen
idiomatisch: improvisieren

I'm not sure what the interviewer is looking for exactly, so I'm going to play it by ear.

to be a sight for sore eyes

wörtlich: ein Anblick für schmerzende Augen sein
idiomatisch: ein erfreulicher Anblick sein;
  eine Augenweide sein

After a long walk in the hot sun,
the ice-cream van was a sight for sore eyes.

Ein schöner Schmerz

Die Redewendung *„to be a sight for sore eyes"* kann man leicht missverstehen. Das tun auch viele englische Muttersprachler. Damit ist gemeint, dass der Anblick die Schmerzen in den Augen lindern kann, und nicht, dass er die Schmerzen in den Augen verursacht! Diese Wendung vermeiden Sie also besser, wenn Sie etwa ein totes Tier am Straßenrand sehen…

to be up to your eyes in something

wörtlich: bis auf die Augen in etwas sein

idiomatisch: bis über beide Ohren in etwas stecken

Luke won't be able to come to the party.
He's still up to his eyes in work.

to keep your eyes peeled for something

wörtlich: nach etwas die Augen geschält halten

idiomatisch: die Augen offenhalten

The cinema is around here somewhere, so everybody
keep your eyes peeled and shout if you see it.

not to have eyes in the back of your head

wörtlich: keine Augen in deinem Hinterkopf haben

idiomatisch: hinten keine Augen haben

How was I supposed to know your mother was standing
behind me when I was criticizing her cooking?
I don't have eyes in the back of my head.

not to see eye to eye with somebody on something

wörtlich: mit jemandem über etwas nicht Auge zu Auge
  sehen

idiomatisch: über etwas anderer Meinung als jemand sein

Her parents don't see eye to eye with each other on Brexit.
They can't stop arguing about it.

to turn a blind eye to something

wörtlich: einer Sache ein blindes Auge zuwenden
idiomatisch: bei etwas ein Auge zudrücken

My season ticket is out of date, but hopefully the ticket inspector will turn a blind eye to it and not make me get off the train.

to raise a few eyebrows

wörtlich: einige Augenbrauen hochziehen
idiomatisch: für Stirnrunzeln sorgen

The school has decided to ban all parents from parking in front of the school gates. That will raise a few eyebrows.

Alles klar?

Hört man den Satz „*to keep your eyes peeled*",
dann ist damit gemeint:

a) *Man sollte auch mal ein Auge zudrücken.*
b) *Man sollte achtsam sein.*
c) *Man sollte die Meinung der anderen anhören.*

 to talk until you are blue in the face

wörtlich: reden bis man blau im Gesicht ist

idiomatisch: sich den Mund fusselig reden

You can talk until you are blue in the face, but I'm not going to change my mind about marrying the man I love.

to be tearing your hair out

wörtlich: sich die Haare rausreißen

idiomatisch: sich die Haare raufen

The leading actor had obviously still not learned his lines and the poor director was tearing his hair out.

 to keep your hair on

wörtlich: deine Haare aufbehalten

idiomatisch: sich wieder abregen; sich nicht aufregen

"Dad, can I have some money for some new shoes?"
"New shoes? You must be joking! I bought you five new pairs only last week!" "Okay, keep your hair on!"

to fall head over heels in love with somebody

wörtlich: Kopf über Fersen mit jemandem in Liebe fallen

idiomatisch: sich bis über beide Ohren in jemanden verlieben

David had always wanted to be a monk,
but then he fell head over heels in love with Amanda.

off the top of your head
wörtlich: von oben auf deinem Kopf weg
idiomatisch: aus dem Stegreif

I can't remember his name off the top of my head.
I'll have to check it out and email it to you later.

 ### to laugh your head off
wörtlich: deinen Kopf ablachen
idiomatisch: sich kaputtlachen; sich totlachen

The clowns came into the circus ring and all the children
were soon laughing their heads off.

– to fall head over heels in love with somebody –

to give somebody a piece of your mind

wörtlich: jemandem ein Stück deiner Meinung geben

idiomatisch: jemandem gründlich die Meinung sagen;
  mit jemandem Tacheles reden

*"Our next-door neighbour said that we were going to
have to chop down those trees." "He said what? Right,
I'm going round there to give him a piece of my mind."*

 ### the mind boggles

wörtlich: der Verstand stutzt

idiomatisch: sich etwas kaum vorstellen können;
  die Vorstellungskraft überschreiten

*Some professional footballers are paid nearly
half a million pounds a week? The mind boggles!*

to take the words out of somebody's mouth

wörtlich: jemandem die Wörter aus dem Mund nehmen

idiomatisch: jemandem das Wort aus dem Mund nehmen

*"What shall we do now?" "How about going to the pub
for a quick pint?" "You took the words right out of my
mouth. I'm dying for a beer."*

 ### to get it in the neck

wörtlich: es im Genick bekommen

idiomatisch: eins aufs Dach / auf die Nase bekommen

*If the boss finds out that you've been cheating the
customers, I'll be the one that gets it in the neck, not you!*

to look down your nose
at somebody / something

wörtlich: auf jemanden / etwas die Nase hinunterblicken
idiomatisch: von jemandem / etwas nichts halten

Sarah's new boyfriend is lovely, but her mum looks down her nose at him because he didn't go to university.

to turn your nose up at something

wörtlich: zu etwas die Nase nach oben richten
idiomatisch: über etwas die Nase rümpfen

I suggested going on a camping holiday to the west of Scotland in November, but my husband just turned his nose up at the idea.

Der kleine große Unterschied

Einige deutsche und englische Redewendungen sind fast identisch, doch die scheinbar unwichtigen Unterschiede darf man nicht vergessen! In *„to take the words out of somebody's mouth"* verwendet man *„words"* im Plural und nicht im Singular wie im Deutschen.

Komisch, dass man in keiner der beiden Sprachen die wahre Anzahl der Wörter berücksichtigt!

to do something by the skin of your teeth

wörtlich: etwas um die Haut deiner Zähne machen

idiomatisch: etwas mit Ach und Krach schaffen;
  etwas mit knapper Not schaffen

*Sophie was late again and only managed to catch
the train by the skin of her teeth.*

to lie through your teeth

wörtlich: durch deine Zähne lügen

idiomatisch: das Blaue vom Himmel herunterlügen;
  nach Strich und Faden lügen

*The detective knew from Gavin's body language
that he was lying through his teeth about the robbery.*

to be on the tip of your tongue

wörtlich: auf deiner Zungenspitze sein

idiomatisch: einem auf der Zunge liegen

*Oh, what's the German word for 'helicopter'?
It's on the tip of my tongue.*

to mean something tongue in cheek

wörtlich: etwas Zunge in Wange meinen

idiomatisch: etwas gar nicht so ernst meinen;
  etwas scherzhaft / augenzwinkernd meinen

*Chris said that nobody could ever find you attractive?
Oh, I'm sure he only meant it tongue in cheek.*

Alles verstanden?

Welche Redewendung passt zu welcher deutschen
Entsprechung? Tragen Sie den Buchstaben der passenden
Übersetzung in das Kästchen ein.

1. ☐ *to play it by ear*

2. ☐ *to be a sight for sore eyes*

3. ☐ *to give somebody a piece of your mind*

4. ☐ *off the top of your head*

5. ☐ *to mean something tongue in cheek*

6. ☐ *to bend somebody's ear*

7. ☐ *to be all ears*

8. ☐ *to keep your eyes peeled for something*

9. ☐ *to keep your hair on*

10. ☐ *to lie through your teeth*

a. eine Augenweide sein **b.** ganz Ohr sein **c.** jemanden
volltexten **d.** das Blaue vom Himmel herunterlügen
e. die Augen offenhalten **f.** aus dem Stegreif **g.** improvisieren
h. sich wieder abregen **i.** etwas scherzhaft meinen
j. jemandem gründlich die Meinung sagen

Am eigenen Leib

to pull somebody's leg
jemanden auf den Arm nehmen

to chance your arm

wörtlich: deinen Arm riskieren

idiomatisch: etwas riskieren; es darauf ankommen lassen

Lauren only had an hour to get to the airport,
so she decided to chance her arm and take a shortcut.

 to cost an arm and a leg

wörtlich: einen Arm und ein Bein kosten

idiomatisch: ein Vermögen kosten; Unsummen kosten

George's new house is absolutely beautiful,
but it must have cost an arm and a leg.

to keep somebody at arm's length

wörtlich: jemanden auf Armeslänge halten

idiomatisch: jemanden auf Distanz halten;
  sich jemanden vom Leib halten

Everyone can see that David adores Katie,
but she prefers to keep him at arm's length.

to twist somebody's arm

wörtlich: jemandem den Arm umdrehen

idiomatisch: jemanden überreden

I'm sure Jack will help me with the decorating if I twist
his arm.

to get off somebody's back
wörtlich: von jemandes Rücken heruntersteigen
idiomatisch: jemanden in Ruhe lassen

*I wish the boss would just get off my back and
give me space to do my job properly.*

to go behind somebody's back
wörtlich: hinter jemandes Rücken gehen
idiomatisch: jemanden hintergehen

*Even though she'd asked her to keep it a secret,
Ruby's sister went behind her back and told their
mother about Ruby losing her job.*

Wertvolle Gliedmaße

Man muss immer ganz genau die Menge und Reihenfolge
beachten, wenn man den übertragenen Sinn einer Redewendung nicht verlieren will. Bei *„to cost an arm and a leg"*
geht es um eine Menge Geld. Das ist schon klar. Aber Menge
und Reihenfolge sind entscheidend. Bei *„to cost a leg and an
arm"* oder *„to cost ten arms and five legs"* besteht die Gefahr,
dass man es wörtlich nimmt!

to keep your fingers crossed

wörtlich: die Finger gekreuzt halten

idiomatisch: die Daumen drücken

I've got an interview at the bank this afternoon.
Keep your fingers crossed for me.

not to be able to put your finger on something

wörtlich: deinen Finger nicht auf etwas legen können

idiomatisch: etwas nicht genau ausmachen können

There was something odd about the scene of the crime,
but Sherlock couldn't put his finger on it.

not to lift a finger to do something

wörtlich: keinen Finger heben, um etwas zu tun

idiomatisch: keinen Finger rühren / krümmen,
  um etwas zu tun

The house was a mess after the party, but she had
to tidy it all up by herself. Her partner didn't lift a finger
to help her.

to pull your finger out

wörtlich: deinen Finger rausziehen

idiomatisch: Dampf machen; Gas geben

You're going to have to really pull your finger out
if you're going to meet that deadline.

to have something at your fingertips

wörtlich: etwas an den Fingerspitzen haben

idiomatisch: etwas in- und auswendig kennen;
etwas aus dem Effeff beherrschen

The saleswoman had all the information about the car at her fingertips.

to find your feet

wörtlich: deine Füße finden

idiomatisch: sich eingewöhnen; Fuß fassen

The first few days in my new job have been difficult, but once I've found my feet, I think I'm going to enjoy it.

Alles klar?

Hört man den Satz „*you need to pull your finger out*",
handelt es sich um …

a) *eine Aufforderung.*

b) *ein Lob.*

c) *eine Absage.*

to keep your feet on the ground
wörtlich: deine Füße auf der Erde halten
idiomatisch: realistisch bleiben; auf dem Boden bleiben

Stacey had a successful career as a top model,
but her family made sure she kept her feet on the ground.

not to put a foot wrong
wörtlich: keinen Fuß falsch setzen
idiomatisch: keinen Fehler machen;
  sich keinen Fehltritt leisten

It was the presenter's first time on live TV and
she was brilliant. She didn't put a foot wrong.

to put your foot down
wörtlich: deinen Fuß hinuntersetzen
idiomatisch: ein Machtwort sprechen

Kyle's dad has put his foot down and told him he can't go
out with his friends in the evening until he's finished his
homework.

to put your foot in it
wörtlich: deinen Fuß reintun
idiomatisch: ins Fettnäpfchen treten

You really put your foot in it asking him about his wife.
Don't you know they got divorced?

to hate somebody's guts

wörtlich: jemandes Eingeweide hassen

idiomatisch: jemanden auf den Tod nicht ausstehen können;
  jemanden nicht riechen können

*My sister has hated my guts ever since I stole her
boyfriend.*

to get your hands on something

wörtlich: deine Hände auf etwas legen

idiomatisch: etwas auftreiben

*Sheila's promised to make me some new curtains if she
can get her hands on some more of that lovely material.*

– not to put a foot wrong –

to give somebody a hand with something

wörtlich: jemandem mit etwas eine Hand geben

idiomatisch: jemandem behilflich sein;
  jemandem zur Hand gehen

Bianca couldn't go to the football match because she'd promised her mum to give her a hand with the gardening.

my heart was in my mouth

wörtlich: mein Herz war in meinem Mund

idiomatisch: mir schlug das Herz bis zum Hals;
  mir rutschte das Herz in die Hose

Joe's heart was in his mouth as the judge announced the winner of the contest.

to drag your heels

wörtlich: deine Fersen schleifen

idiomatisch: sich Zeit lassen; etwas in die Länge ziehen

Work on the new school should have started already, but the council has been dragging its heels as usual over granting permission.

not to have a leg to stand on

wörtlich: kein Bein haben, auf dem man stehen kann

idiomatisch: nichts in der Hand haben

You could try taking the toaster back to the shop, but if you've lost the receipt, you don't have a leg to stand on.

to pull somebody's leg

wörtlich: jemandes Bein ziehen

idiomatisch: jemanden auf den Arm / die Schippe nehmen;
 jemanden durch den Kakao ziehen

*Don't worry. Andy won't really tell anyone your secret.
He's just pulling your leg.*

to give somebody the cold shoulder

wörtlich: jemandem die kalte Schulter geben

idiomatisch: jemandem die kalte Schulter zeigen

*Kate's colleagues have been giving her the cold shoulder
since she told the boss about them sending personal
emails during working hours.*

Take your time!

„To drag your heels" wird immer im negativen Sinn
verwendet. Damit ist gemeint, dass man etwas bewusst
langsam tut und es einem egal ist, wenn dadurch Verzöge-
rungen entstehen. Das steht im Kontrast zu *„to take your
time"*, was auch im positiven Sinn verstanden werden
kann, so wie die ähnliche deutsche Wendung *„sich Zeit
lassen"*. *„Lass dir (ruhig) Zeit!"* also immer mit *„Take your
time!"* übersetzen, nicht mit *„Drag your heels!"*

to have a chip on your shoulder

wörtlich: einen Splitter auf deiner Schulter haben

idiomatisch: einen Komplex haben

Carol has a real chip on her shoulder about never having been to college.

to be under somebody's thumb

wörtlich: unter jemandes Daumen sein

idiomatisch: unter jemandes Fuchtel stehen

Poor old Martin does everything his mother tells him to. He's really under her thumb.

to stick out like a sore thumb

wörtlich: wie ein schmerzender Daumen abstehen

idiomatisch: nicht zu übersehen sein;
auffallen wie ein bunter Hund

Jake stuck out like a sore thumb at the opera in his jeans and T-shirt.

to keep somebody on their toes

wörtlich: jemanden auf den Zehen halten

idiomatisch: jemanden auf Trab / Zack halten

Our maths teacher likes to keep us on our toes by giving us a surprise test every now and then.

Alles verstanden?

Welche Redewendung passt zu welcher deutschen Entsprechung? Tragen Sie den Buchstaben der passenden Übersetzung in das Kästchen ein.

1. ☐ to drag your heels
2. ☐ to twist somebody's arm
3. ☐ to find your feet
4. ☐ to give somebody a hand with something
5. ☐ to put your foot down
6. ☐ to go behind somebody's back
7. ☐ to get off somebody's back
8. ☐ to get your hands on something
9. ☐ to chance your arm
10. ☐ to be under somebody's thumb

a. ein Machtwort sprechen **b.** jemanden hintergehen **c.** es darauf ankommen lassen **d.** unter jemandes Fuchtel stehen **e.** sich eingewöhnen **f.** jemandem behilflich sein **g.** sich Zeit lassen **h.** jemanden in Ruhe lassen **i.** jemanden überreden **j.** etwas auftreiben

In der Natur der Sache

to be barking up the wrong tree
auf dem Holzweg sein

to have your head in the clouds

wörtlich: den Kopf in den Wolken haben

idiomatisch: in den Wolken schweben; Gedanken spinnen

Gordon needs to face reality and get a proper job,
but he still has his head in the clouds all the time.

to live in cloud cuckoo land

wörtlich: im Wolkenkuckucksland leben

idiomatisch: im Wolkenkuckucksheim leben;
  hinter dem Mond leben

If you think you can force me to agree to a divorce,
you're living in cloud cuckoo land.

to be up the creek without a paddle

wörtlich: am Ende des Flüsschens ohne Paddel sein

idiomatisch: in der Tinte sitzen; völlig aufgeschmissen sein

Business was really bad and Joe knew that if the bank
asked him to repay his loans now he'd be up the creek
without a paddle.

to be in seventh heaven

wörtlich: im siebten Himmel sein

idiomatisch: im siebten Himmel sein / schweben

Daniel's in seventh heaven. He just got accepted on
a course to study music in New York.

to move heaven and earth

wörtlich: Himmel und Erde in Bewegung setzen
idiomatisch: Himmel und Hölle in Bewegung setzen

The victim's father swore that he would move heaven and earth to get justice for his daughter.

to see how the land lies

wörtlich: sehen, wie das Land liegt
idiomatisch: die Lage peilen

The housing market is very quiet just now.
Let's wait until the spring and then see how the land lies.

Achtung, unzensiert!

Wenn man sich unverblümt ausdrücken möchte,
kann man auch *„to be up shit creek without a paddle"*
(*„in der Scheiße stecken"*) statt *„to be up the creek"* sagen.

Aber Vorsicht:
Bei den älteren Generationen in den englischsprachigen
Ländern ist das S-Wort immer noch tabu. Also am besten bei
der neutralen Version bleiben.

to be over the moon
wörtlich: über dem Mond sein
idiomatisch: überglücklich sein; hin und weg sein

Katrina's parents were over the moon when she told them she was pregnant.

to make a mountain out of a molehill
wörtlich: aus einem Maulwurfshügel einen Berg machen
idiomatisch: aus einer Mücke einen Elefanten machen

If you've forgotten your mobile, you can just borrow mine. Don't make a mountain out of a molehill.

to be a drop in the ocean
wörtlich: ein Tropfen im Meer sein
idiomatisch: ein Tropfen auf den heißen Stein sein

The government wants to introduce stricter laws about diesel cars, but it'll just be a drop in the ocean in the fight against climate change.

to be raining cats and dogs
wörtlich: Katzen und Hunde regnen
idiomatisch: in Strömen regnen; wie aus Kübeln gießen

It was raining cats and dogs when I set off for work and I was wet through by the time I arrived.

to sell somebody down the river

wörtlich: jemanden den Fluss hinunterverkaufen
idiomatisch: jemanden verschaukeln;
  jemanden auf den Arm nehmen

Alistair realized too late that his business partner had joined a rival company and sold him down the river.

to be on the rocks

wörtlich: auf den Felsen sein
idiomatisch: am Ende sein; in die Brüche zu gehen drohen

There are rumours in the press that the footballer's marriage is on the rocks.

Alles klar?

David ist mit seinem neuen Job sehr zufrieden.
Wie drückt er das aus?

a) *I'm spaced out about my new job.*
b) *I'm out of this world about my new job.*
c) *I'm over the moon about my new job.*

to be all at sea
wörtlich: völlig auf See sein
idiomatisch: nicht mehr weiterwissen; ratlos sein

Without the leadership of their captain,
the rest of the team were all at sea.

the sky's the limit
wörtlich: der Himmel ist die Grenze
idiomatisch: nach oben sind keine Grenzen gesetzt;
  alles ist möglich

With your beauty and my brains, the sky's the limit!

to be a slippery slope
wörtlich: ein glitschiger Hang sein
idiomatisch: ein gefährlicher Weg sein

Andy started drinking in his teens and it was a slippery
slope. By the time he was 25 he was an alcoholic.

to get the wrong end of the stick
wörtlich: das falsche Ende des Stocks erwischen
idiomatisch: etwas völlig falsch verstehen;
  etwas in die falsche Kehle bekommen

Charlie didn't say you were fat.
You've got the wrong end of the stick.

 to give somebody some stick

wörtlich: jemandem etwas Stock geben

idiomatisch: jemandem die Leviten lesen

If I don't finish painting the fence today,
my dad's going to give me some stick.

to be a storm in a teacup

wörtlich: ein Sturm in einer Teetasse sein

idiomatisch: ein Sturm im Wasserglas sein

Those neighbours are always arguing about something,
but it's usually a storm in a teacup.

– to be a storm in a teacup –

to steal somebody's thunder

wörtlich: jemandes Donner stehlen
idiomatisch: jemandem die Schau stehlen;
  jemandem den Wind aus den Segeln nehmen

*The minister kept his own speech short because he didn't
want to steal the president's thunder.*

to be barking up the wrong tree

wörtlich: den falschen Baum hinaufbellen
idiomatisch: auf dem Holzweg / falschen Dampfer sein

*The police have arrested Mr Jones for the murder,
but I think they may be barking up the wrong tree.*

not to grow on trees

wörtlich: nicht auf Bäumen wachsen
idiomatisch: nicht vom Himmel fallen
  (meist: Geld fällt nicht vom Himmel)

*No, you can't have another new dress for the party.
Money doesn't grow on trees, you know!*

to be on the crest of a wave

wörtlich: auf dem Kamm einer Welle sein
idiomatisch: ganz oben sein / schwimmen

*It had taken a lot of hard work to win this contract, but
now the designer felt like he was on the crest of a wave.*

to get wind of something

wörtlich: Wind von etwas bekommen

idiomatisch: von etwas Wind bekommen

The residents got wind of a plan to build a motorway through the housing estate and decided to organize a protest.

not to be able to see the wood for the trees

wörtlich: den Wald wegen der Bäume nicht sehen können

idiomatisch: den Wald vor lauter Bäumen nicht sehen

The police had gathered so much evidence and information about the crime that it was hard to see the wood for the trees.

Auf dem Holzweg

Ein bellender Hund unter einem Baum, womöglich ein selbstgefälliges Eichhörnchen in einem anderen. Die Redewendung *„to be barking up the wrong tree"* beschwört lustige Bilder im Kopf herauf. Obwohl es den Ausdruck im Deutschen so nicht gibt, ist er aufgrund seiner Anschaulichkeit verständlich: Der Hund bellt den falschen Baum an, er ist also *„auf dem Holzweg"*.

Man darf aber nicht vergessen, den Baum zu erwähnen, denn *„you are barking"* allein bedeutet *„du spinnst"*!

Touch wood!
wörtlich: Berühre Holz!
idiomatisch: Toi, toi, toi!

The weather is going to be hot and sunny on the day of the festival. Touch wood!

not to be out of the woods yet
wörtlich: noch nicht aus dem Wald sein
idiomatisch: noch nicht über den Berg sein; noch nicht aus dem Schneider sein

The doctors said that the operation was a success but that Alice was still very weak, so she's not out of the woods yet.

 ## to be out of this world
wörtlich: außerhalb dieser Welt sein
idiomatisch: fantastisch sein

The restaurant itself wasn't particularly attractive, but the food was out of this world.

to mean the world to somebody
wörtlich: jemandem die Welt bedeuten
idiomatisch: jemandem alles bedeuten; jemandes Ein und Alles sein

Mum misses you so much. It would mean the world to her if you were to call her on her birthday.

Alles verstanden?

Welche Redewendung passt zu welcher deutschen Entsprechung? Tragen Sie den Buchstaben der passenden Übersetzung in das Kästchen ein.

1. ☐ *to be a storm in a teacup*
2. ☐ *to be on the crest of a wave*
3. ☐ *to be all at sea*
4. ☐ *to get the wrong end of the stick*
5. ☐ *to be barking up the wrong tree*
6. ☐ *the sky's the limit*
7. ☐ *to be over the moon*
8. ☐ *to be a drop in the ocean*
9. ☐ *to steal somebody's thunder*
10. ☐ *to be up the creek without a paddle*

a. ein Tropfen auf den heißen Stein sein **b.** alles ist möglich **c.** auf dem Holzweg sein **d.** ganz oben sein **e.** überglücklich sein **f.** in der Tinte sitzen **g.** ein Sturm im Wasserglas sein **h.** jemandem die Schau stehlen **i.** nicht mehr weiterwissen **j.** etwas in die falsche Kehle bekommen

Lifestyler

to get too big for your boots
langsam größenwahnsinnig werden

to be on the ball

wörtlich: am Ball sein

idiomatisch: auf Zack / Draht sein

That's the second time I've dialled a wrong number.
I'm just not on the ball this morning at all.

to keep your eye on the ball

wörtlich: dein Auge am Ball halten

idiomatisch: sich (auf die Hauptsache) konzentrieren

Rock climbing can be dangerous, but as long
as you keep your eye on the ball and don't get distracted,
you'll be fine.

to ring a bell

wörtlich: eine Glocke läuten

idiomatisch: einem bekannt vorkommen;
  jemandem etwas sagen

"Do you remember Dave Williams from school?"
"No, sorry. That name doesn't ring a bell."

to have a bee in your bonnet

wörtlich: eine Biene in deiner Haube haben

idiomatisch: einen Tick / Spleen haben

Mr Robinson has a bee in his bonnet about his
neighbours playing loud music.

to be able to read somebody like a book

wörtlich: jemanden wie ein Buch lesen können
idiomatisch: in jemandem wie in einem Buch lesen können

I tried to hide my disappointment, but Mum read me like a book and knew that something was wrong.

to get too big for your boots

wörtlich: zu groß für deine Stiefel werden
idiomatisch: langsam größenwahnsinnig werden

That manager has started criticizing everyone's work. He's getting a bit too big for his boots.

Bienen statt Zecken

Auch wenn eine Dame heutzutage keine Haube mehr trägt, ist die Redewendung *„to have a bee in your bonnet"* immer noch gebräuchlich. Das Bild sollte man sich gut einprägen, denn wenn man nicht aufpasst und versucht, die deutsche Übersetzung *„einen Tick haben"* wortwörtlich ins Englische zu übersetzen, kommt man fälschlicherweise auf *„to have a tick"*, also *„eine Zecke haben"*.

 to give somebody the boot
wörtlich: jemandem den Stiefel geben
idiomatisch: jemanden rausschmeißen;
  jemanden in die Wüste schicken

*The actor was terrible and it wasn't long before
the director was forced to give him the boot.*

to have another card up your sleeve
wörtlich: noch eine Karte oben im Ärmel haben
idiomatisch: noch einen Trumpf in der Hand haben;
  noch etwas in der Hinterhand haben

*So far the negotiations were going badly,
but the government still had another card up its sleeve.*

to be a chip off the old block
wörtlich: ein Splitter vom alten Block sein
idiomatisch: der Apfel fällt nicht weit vom Stamm;
  ganz der Vater sein

*Billy's son is also a talented footballer.
He's a real chip off the old block.*

to be as fit as a fiddle
wörtlich: so fit wie eine Fiedel sein
idiomatisch: kerngesund sein; fit wie ein Turnschuh sein

*My grandfather may be in his eighties, but he's still
as fit as a fiddle.*

to beat somebody at their own game

wörtlich: jemanden bei seinem eigenen Spiel schlagen

idiomatisch: jemanden mit seinen eigenen Waffen schlagen

Local shops are cutting prices to try to beat the
supermarkets at their own game.

to give the game away

wörtlich: das Spiel weggeben

idiomatisch: alles verraten / ausplaudern

Don't give him too many hints or
you'll give the game away.

Alles klar?

Hört man *„the team should give their coach the boot"*,
dann ist damit gemeint:

a) *Das Team sollte sich einen neuen Trainer suchen.*
b) *Das Team sollte seinem Trainer gratulieren.*
c) *Das Team hat seinem Trainer seinen Erfolg zu verdanken.*

to do something at the drop of a hat
wörtlich: etwas beim Fallenlassen eines Huts machen
idiomatisch: etwas auf der Stelle machen;
  etwas ohne zu zögern machen

*Sandy would move house at the drop of a hat
if he could afford to.*

I take my hat off to him
wörtlich: ich ziehe vor ihm meinen Hut
idiomatisch: Hut ab!

*My neighbour is eighty but still goes out jogging.
I take my hat off to him.*

to be as high as a kite
wörtlich: so hoch wie ein Drachen sein
idiomatisch: völlig aufgedreht sein; high sein

*Paula got a valentine's card from Andy and
was as high as a kite for the rest of the week.*

to have lost your marbles
wörtlich: deine Murmeln verloren haben
idiomatisch: nicht alle Tassen im Schrank haben;
  den Verstand verloren haben

*I heard the boss talking to himself again.
I think he might have lost his marbles.*

to be music to somebody's ears

wörtlich: Musik zu jemandes Ohren sein
idiomatisch: Musik in jemandes Ohren sein

The exam has been cancelled? That's music to my ears!

to face the music

wörtlich: sich der Musik stellen
idiomatisch: für etwas geradestehen;
  die Konsequenzen tragen

*Everyone already knows it was you who set off the fire
alarm, so it's time for you to face the music.*

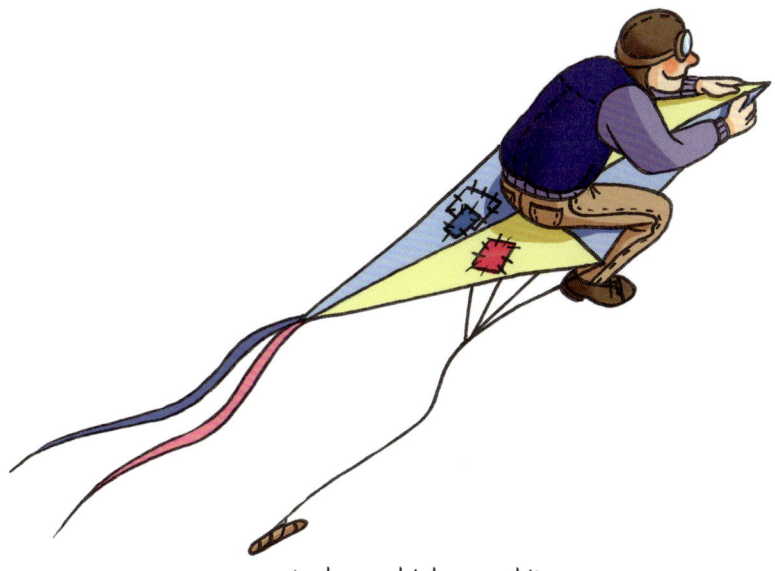

– to be as high as a kite –

to be no oil painting

wörtlich: kein Ölgemälde sein

idiomatisch: nicht gerade eine Schönheit sein

Women must be attracted to him because of his money because he's certainly no oil painting.

I wouldn't like to be in your shoes

wörtlich: ich möchte nicht in deinen Schuhen sein

idiomatisch: ich möchte nicht in deiner Haut stecken /
  an deiner Stelle sein

I wouldn't like to be in your shoes when your dad gets home and sees you've broken the window.

to get your skates on

wörtlich: deine Schlittschuhe anziehen

idiomatisch: ein bisschen dalli machen; einen Zahn zulegen

*If Kelly doesn't get her skates on,
she'll miss the train again.*

to pull your socks up

wörtlich: deine Socken hochziehen

idiomatisch: sich am Riemen reißen

*Danny needs to pull his socks up at school or
he's not going to get any qualifications.*

 ## to put a sock in it

wörtlich: eine Socke reintun

idiomatisch: die Klappe halten; die Luft anhalten

"My dad's richer than your dad!"
"Oh, put a sock in it!"

to be on song

wörtlich: auf Lied sein

idiomatisch: in Hochform sein

It was a difficult presentation to make,
but Gavin was right on song.

Bitte recht ungenau!

„*To get your skates on*" stammt aus einer Zeit, als die einzigen „*skates*" für das Eis bestimmt waren. Rollschuhe und Inlineskates waren damals noch Zukunftsmusik. Bei den meisten Redewendungen ist es wichtig, genau zu sein. In diesem Fall jedoch funktioniert die Redewendung nur, wenn man von sehr ungenauen „*skates*" spricht.

to make a song and dance about something

wörtlich: ein Lied und einen Tanz über etwas machen

idiomatisch: wegen etwas ein großes Theater / Trara machen

Tony was only five minutes late,
but his mum made a big song and dance about it.

to wear the trousers

wörtlich: die Hosen tragen

idiomatisch: die Hosen anhaben

Sarah's husband is so shy and quiet. It's obvious
who wears the trousers in their house.

to blow your own trumpet

wörtlich: deine eigene Trompete blasen

idiomatisch: sich selbst loben; sich selbst beweihräuchern

I don't like to blow my own trumpet, but that's
the fourth time I've won a prize for my poetry.

to change your tune

wörtlich: deine Melodie ändern

idiomatisch: seine Meinung ändern;
  einen anderen Ton anschlagen

David's changed his tune!
He always said he never wanted to live in the city.

Alles verstanden?

Welche Redewendung passt zu welcher deutschen Entsprechung? Tragen Sie den Buchstaben der passenden Übersetzung in das Kästchen ein.

1. ☐ *to face the music*
2. ☐ *to be on song*
3. ☐ *to pull your socks up*
4. ☐ *to have lost your marbles*
5. ☐ *to give the game away*
6. ☐ *to be no oil painting*
7. ☐ *to be as fit as a fiddle*
8. ☐ *to give somebody the boot*
9. ☐ *to blow your own trumpet*
10. ☐ *to change your tune*

a. jemanden in die Wüste schicken **b.** seine Meinung ändern **c.** sich am Riemen reißen **d.** alles verraten **e.** sich selbst loben **f.** nicht gerade eine Schönheit sein **g.** nicht alle Tassen im Schrank haben **h.** in Hochform sein **i.** fit wie ein Turnschuh sein **j.** für etwas geradestehen

Farbe bekennen

to be tickled pink
sich wie ein Schneekönig freuen

to come out of the blue
wörtlich: aus dem Blauen kommen
idiomatisch: aus heiterem Himmel kommen

The job offer came out of the blue. Nobody was as surprised as Jack when he read the letter.

 ### to do something until you're blue in the face
wörtlich: etwas machen, bis du blau im Gesicht bist
idiomatisch: etwas bis zum Gehtnichtmehr machen

You can argue with Dave until you're blue in the face, but he'll never admit he's wrong.

to pass something with flying colours
wörtlich: etwas mit fliegenden Farben bestehen
idiomatisch: etwas mit Bravur / Glanz und Gloria bestehen

Ed passed his A levels with flying colours and is now studying at Cambridge.

to get thrown in at the deep end
wörtlich: am tiefen Ende hineingeworfen werden
idiomatisch: ins kalte Wasser geworfen werden

This company believes in throwing new recruits in at the deep end. You will be dealing directly with our customers from day one.

 to pull a fast one on somebody

wörtlich: jemandem einen Schnellen überziehen

idiomatisch: jemanden übers Ohr hauen

It was only when he read the contract later that Sam realized that the lawyer had pulled a fast one on him. But by then it was too late.

to be worth your weight in gold

wörtlich: dein Gewicht in Gold wert sein

idiomatisch: nicht mit Gold aufzuwiegen sein

A personal assistant with Sandra's experience is worth her weight in gold to a manager.

Gefühle an Farben erkennen

Die falsche Farbe in einer Redewendung kann leicht Verwirrung stiften. Das Blau in *„to do something until you're blue in the face"* deutet darauf hin, dass man fast am Ersticken ist, weil man so lange versucht hat, etwas zu tun. *„Red in the face"* aber deutet auf physische Bewegung, Zorn oder Peinlichkeit hin, während es bei *„to go green"* eher um Neid oder Übelkeit geht.

to have a heart of gold

wörtlich: ein Herz aus Gold haben

idiomatisch: ein Herz aus Gold haben

My grandma will do anything to help other people.
She has a real heart of gold.

to be green with envy

wörtlich: grün vor Neid sein

idiomatisch: grün vor Neid sein; vor Neid platzen

Sophie was green with envy when she saw
the new bike her sister had got for Christmas.

the grass is always greener (on the other side)

wörtlich: das Gras (auf der anderen Seite) ist immer grüner

idiomatisch: die Kirschen in Nachbars Garten
  schmecken süßer

"I wish I could leave my job and open a restaurant
like you." "The grass is always greener on the other side.
You don't have to work long hours like I do."

to make light work of something

wörtlich: aus etwas leichte Arbeit machen

idiomatisch: mit etwas spielend fertig werden

Angus made light work of arranging the holiday.
It only took a couple of emails and everything was booked.

to be a long shot

wörtlich: ein langer Schuss sein
idiomatisch: wenig Aussicht auf Erfolg haben

The treasure might be buried in this field.
I know it's a long shot, but we have to try to find it.

to cut a long story short

wörtlich: um eine lange Geschichte zu kürzen
idiomatisch: langer Rede kurzer Sinn

To cut a long story short, the robbers escaped
to Brazil with the money and lived in luxury for
the rest of their lives.

Alles klar?

Verwendet man den Satz „*the grass is always
greener (on the other side)*", will man damit sagen:

a) *Man sollte nicht so schnell neidisch sein.*
b) *Man hat vergessen, den Rasen zu sprengen.*
c) *Man hat wenig Aussicht auf Erfolg.*

to be in the pink
wörtlich: im Rosa sein
idiomatisch: gesund und munter sein

Grandad hasn't been well,
but after a fortnight in hospital he's in the pink again.

 ### to be tickled pink
wörtlich: rosa gekitzelt sein
idiomatisch: sich wie ein Schneekönig freuen

I was tickled pink by the boss's email.
Maybe he does appreciate my work after all!

 ### to do something on the quiet
wörtlich: etwas auf der Stille tun
idiomatisch: etwas still und heimlich machen

She's trying to lose weight but keeps eating packets
of chocolate biscuits on the quiet.

to be in the red
wörtlich: im Roten sein
idiomatisch: in den roten Zahlen sein; in den Miesen sein

After the disappointing Christmas sales, the company
was back in the red.

to catch somebody red-handed
wörtlich: jemanden mit roten Händen erwischen
idiomatisch: jemanden auf frischer Tat / in flagranti ertappen

The robber was caught red-handed trying to open the safe.

to go as red as a beetroot
wörtlich: so rot wie eine Rote Bete werden
idiomatisch: rot werden wie eine Tomate

Whenever Simon speaks to you,
you always go as red as a beetroot.

– to be in the pink –

to take the rough with the smooth
wörtlich: das Raue mit der Glätte nehmen
idiomatisch: das Leben nehmen, wie es kommt

You can't always expect everything to go as planned.
You just have to take the rough with the smooth.

to give somebody short shrift
wörtlich: jemandem kurze Beichte geben
idiomatisch: jemanden kurz abfertigen

James has tried to discuss the issue,
but his brother always just gives him short shrift.

to be slow on the uptake
wörtlich: langsam bei der Aufnahme sein
idiomatisch: eine lange Leitung haben;
  schwer von Begriff sein

Oh, you have to switch the computer on first?
Sorry, I'm a bit slow on the uptake.

 ## to be a soft touch
wörtlich: eine weiche Berührung sein
idiomatisch: leicht rumzukriegen sein

Ella's dad tries to be strict with her,
but her mum is such a soft touch that Ella knows
she'll let her do anything she wants.

to have a soft spot for somebody
wörtlich: eine weiche Stelle für jemanden haben
idiomatisch: eine Schwäche / ein Faible für jemanden haben

Alan offered to help you carry your bags to the car again?
I think he has a soft spot for you.

to be a square peg in a round hole
wörtlich: ein quadratischer Pflock in einem runden Loch
  sein
idiomatisch: sich völlig fehl am Platz fühlen

Nobody else in my class is interested in the same things
as I am. I feel like I'm a square peg in a round hole.

Shrift ≠ Schrift

Das englische Wort „*shrift*" hört man heutzutage nur noch
in der Redewendung „*to give somebody short shrift*". Früher
wurde das Verb „*to shrive*" verwendet, um die Abnahme
der Beichte und die Erteilung der Absolution durch einen
Priester zu beschreiben – heute sagt man „*to confess*" bzw.
„*confession*". Mit dem deutschen Wort „*Schrift*" hat „*shrift*"
also nichts zu tun.

 to be as thick as two short planks

wörtlich: so dicht wie zwei kurze Latten sein

idiomatisch: dumm wie Bohnenstroh sein

There's no point in asking my brother to help me with my homework. He's as thick as two short planks.

to vanish into thin air

wörtlich: in dünne Luft verschwinden

idiomatisch: sich in Luft auflösen

I parked the car in front of the office this morning and now it's vanished into thin air.

to pull your weight

wörtlich: dein Gewicht ziehen

idiomatisch: seinen Beitrag leisten

Gary isn't pulling his weight at work and his colleagues are starting to complain to the boss about him.

to be as white as a sheet

wörtlich: so weiß wie ein Bettlaken sein

idiomatisch: kreidebleich sein

*After hearing about the accident,
Tom was as white as a sheet.*

Alles verstanden?

Welche Redewendung passt zu welcher deutschen
Entsprechung? Tragen Sie den Buchstaben der passenden
Übersetzung in das Kästchen ein.

1. ☐ *to be as white as a sheet*

2. ☐ *to be in the red*

3. ☐ *to be a square peg in a round hole*

4. ☐ *to come out of the blue*

5. ☐ *to be green with envy*

6. ☐ *to be tickled pink*

7. ☐ *to vanish into thin air*

8. ☐ *to be worth your weight in gold*

9. ☐ *to be a soft touch*

10. ☐ *to catch somebody red-handed*

a. aus heiterem Himmel kommen **b.** kreidebleich sein
c. sich wie ein Schneekönig freuen **d.** in den Miesen sein
e. sich in Luft auflösen **f.** jemanden auf frischer Tat ertappen
g. vor Neid platzen **h.** sich völlig fehl am Platz fühlen
i. nicht mit Gold aufzuwiegen sein **j.** leicht rumzukriegen sein

Zahltag!

to be back to square one
wieder von vorn anfangen müssen

into the bargain
wörtlich: in den Handel
idiomatisch: darüber hinaus; obendrein

*The new shop has a big range of products and
they're all really cheap into the bargain.*

to get more bang for your buck
wörtlich: mehr Knall für deinen Dollar kriegen
idiomatisch: mehr für sein Geld kriegen

*This car model is the same price but comes with
lots of extras so you get more bang for your buck.*

to cost a packet
wörtlich: ein Paket kosten
idiomatisch: ein Heidengeld kosten

*Nick just bought himself a private jet.
That must have cost a packet!*

to feel like a million dollars
wörtlich: sich wie eine Million Dollar fühlen
idiomatisch: sich sauwohl fühlen; Bäume ausreißen können

*I finally got a good night's sleep last night and
this morning I feel like a million dollars.*

you can bet your bottom dollar

wörtlich: du kannst um deinen untersten Dollar wetten

idiomatisch: du kannst Gift darauf nehmen

It's Mum's birthday next week and you can bet your bottom dollar that Dad will forget again.

first come, first served

wörtlich: als Erster gekommen, als Erster bedient

idiomatisch: wer zuerst kommt, mahlt zuerst

Tickets to the concert will be available on a first come, first served basis.

Eine einheitliche Währung?

„To feel like a million dollars" und „you can bet your bottom dollar" sind in allen englischsprachigen Ländern gebräuchlich, auch wenn sie den Dollar nicht als Währung haben. Geldwechseln ist nicht nötig. Der Londoner Gentleman mit seiner neuen Melone sagt „I feel like a million dollars!", genauso wie der Cowboy in Texas mit seinem neuen Cowboyhut.

93

 to be not half bad

wörtlich: nicht halb schlecht sein

idiomatisch: gar nicht so übel sein

This wine isn't half bad.
I think we should buy another bottle.

 to go halves (with someone) on something

wörtlich: (mit jemandem) auf etwas Hälften gehen

idiomatisch: (mit jemandem) bei etwas halbe-halbe machen

My brother and I have decided to go halves on
a camera as a present for Dad's birthday.

 Not half!

wörtlich: Nicht halb!

idiomatisch: Und ob!

"Thank you for digging the garden. Would you
like a nice cold beer?" "Not half!"

not to do things by halves

wörtlich: Sachen nicht um Hälften machen

idiomatisch: keine halben Sachen machen

Kathryn has invited 500 guests to her wedding.
She doesn't do things by halves!

 never in a million years

wörtlich: nie in einer Million Jahren

idiomatisch: nie im Leben; im Leben nicht

I would never have believed he was the killer.
Never in a million years.

to talk nineteen to the dozen

wörtlich: neunzehn zum Dutzend reden

idiomatisch: wie ein Wasserfall reden

The tour guide was talking nineteen to the dozen and
it was difficult to follow what she was saying.

Alles klar?

Dein Bruder meint: „*That new goalkeeper isn't half bad.*"
Ist dein Bruder …

a) *wegen des neuen Torhüters verzweifelt?*
b) *mit dem neuen Torhüter zufrieden?*
c) *von dem neuen Torhüter enttäuscht?*

to be back to square one

wörtlich: zurück zu Feld Eins sein

idiomatisch: wieder von vorn anfangen müssen;
  wieder am Nullpunkt angelangt sein

*None of the banks wanted to give us a loan for
our business so we were back to square one.*

in for a penny, in for a pound

wörtlich: drin für einen Penny, drin für ein Pfund

idiomatisch: wenn schon, denn schon

*You want to invite another thirty people to the party?
Okay. In for a penny, in for a pound.*

the penny dropped

wörtlich: der Penny fiel

idiomatisch: der Groschen ist gefallen

*When Natasha found texts from another woman
on her husband's phone, the penny dropped.*

on second thoughts

wörtlich: auf zweiten Gedanken

idiomatisch: wenn ich es mir recht überlege

*Let's drive into London at the weekend.
On second thoughts, let's take the train.*

to be second nature to somebody

wörtlich: jemandem zweite Natur sein
idiomatisch: jemandem zur zweiten Natur geworden sein

Emma had been a hairdresser for so long that cutting hair was second nature to her.

to talk shop

wörtlich: Laden reden
idiomatisch: fachsimpeln; sich über die Arbeit unterhalten

I hate going to the pub with you and your colleagues from work. You just talk shop the whole time.

– to talk shop –

97

to be at sixes and sevens

wörtlich: bei Sechsen und Siebenen sein

idiomatisch: völlig durcheinander sein;
  drunter und drüber gehen

*Four of their employees left suddenly last week
so they're all at sixes and sevens this week.*

to be six of one and half a dozen of the other

wörtlich: sechs von der einen (Sorte) und
  ein halbes Dutzend von der anderen sein

idiomatisch: Jacke wie Hose sein; gehupft wie gesprungen sein

*"Shall we take the coast road or go across country?"
"It's six of one and half a dozen of the other. It will take
us just as long either way."*

to be the sixty-four thousand dollar question

wörtlich: die vierundsechszigtausend Dollar Frage sein

idiomatisch: die Preisfrage / Gretchenfrage sein

*It's clear that the town needs a new hospital.
But who's going to pay for it?
That's the sixty-four thousand dollar question.*

to be ten a penny

wörtlich: zehn Stück pro Penny sein

idiomatisch: es gibt sie wie Sand am Meer

*We don't need another supermarket.
They're ten a penny around here.*

to do a roaring trade in something

wörtlich: ein brüllendes Geschäft in etwas machen

idiomatisch: ein Riesengeschäft mit etwas machen

The bookshop was doing a roaring trade in the scandalous new biography of the prime minister.

to be in a Catch-22 situation

wörtlich: in einer Haken-22 Situation sein

idiomatisch: in der Zwickmühle sitzen

If Michael doesn't pay his rent, he'll be thrown out of his flat. But then, if he does pay it, he won't be able to pay his university fees. He's in a real Catch-22 situation.

Irrelevant oder einfach nur unschlüssig?

Mit „*it's six of one and half a dozen of the other*" ist gemeint, dass zwei Möglichkeiten identisch sind. Wenn es sich irgendwie vermeiden lässt, verwenden Sie diese Redewendung also nicht beim Einkaufen. Und besonders nicht beim Einkaufen von zwölf Eiern von zwei verschiedenen Sorten. Da hält Sie der Verkäufer vermutlich für total unschlüssig und bedient Sie nicht.

to be in two minds about something
wörtlich: über etwas in zwei Meinungen sein
idiomatisch: sich unschlüssig sein

*Paul's parents were in two minds about
which school to send him to.*

to put two and two together
wörtlich: zwei und zwei zusammenstellen
idiomatisch: zwei und zwei zusammenzählen

*When he saw the broken window,
Monty put two and two together and called the police.*

two can play at that game
wörtlich: zwei können das Spiel spielen
idiomatisch: wie du mir, so ich dir

*Sandra hasn't invited me to her wedding?
Well, two can play at that game. I'm not going to invite
her to mine.*

two's company, three's a crowd
wörtlich: zwei sind Gesellschaft, drei sind eine
  Menschenmenge
idiomatisch: drei sind einer zu viel

*My sister and her new boyfriend invited me to go on
holiday with them but I said no. Two's company and
three's a crowd.*

Alles verstanden?

Welche Redewendung passt zu welcher deutschen Entsprechung? Tragen Sie den Buchstaben der passenden Übersetzung in das Kästchen ein.

1. ☐ *to be in a Catch-22 situation*
2. ☐ *to put two and two together*
3. ☐ *you can bet your bottom dollar*
4. ☐ *into the bargain*
5. ☐ *two's company, three's a crowd*
6. ☐ *to be at sixes and sevens*
7. ☐ *to talk nineteen to the dozen*
8. ☐ *to get more bang for your buck*
9. ☐ *two can play at that game*
10. ☐ *to be ten a penny*

a. drei sind einer zu viel **b.** wie ein Wasserfall reden
c. darüber hinaus **d.** zwei und zwei zusammenzählen
e. wie du mir, so ich dir **f.** in einer Zwickmühle sitzen
g. es gibt sie wie Sand am Meer **h.** völlig durcheinander
sein **i.** mehr für sein Geld kriegen **j.** du kannst Gift darauf
nehmen

Traum vom Eigenheim

to sit on the fence
sich neutral verhalten

to be water under the bridge
wörtlich: Wasser unter der Brücke sein
idiomatisch: Schnee von gestern sein

*Tim and Alex fell out about money many years ago.
But that's all water under the bridge now.*

to cross that bridge when you come to it
wörtlich: jene Brücke überqueren, wenn du sie erreichst
idiomatisch: alles zu seiner Zeit; kommt Zeit, kommt Rat

*Let's not worry just now about which removal company
we're going to use. We'll cross that bridge when we
come to it.*

 ## to kick the bucket
wörtlich: den Eimer treten
idiomatisch: den Löffel abgeben; ins Gras beißen

*John's grandad was only thirty
when he kicked the bucket.*

to build castles in the air
wörtlich: Schlösser in der Luft bauen
idiomatisch: Luftschlösser bauen

*The manager thinks his team will be in the Champions
League next season, but he's just building castles in the air.*

to run like clockwork

wörtlich: wie Uhrwerk laufen

idiomatisch: wie am Schnürchen laufen

Thanks to Stewart for organizing the golf tournament. The whole thing ran like clockwork.

to have skeletons in the closet

wörtlich: Skelette im Schrank haben

idiomatisch: Leichen im Keller haben

They seemed to be a nice family, but it turned out that they had quite a few skeletons in the closet.

Stilvoll ableben

Die falsche Stilebene einer Redewendung kann sehr verletzend sein, besonders wenn es um ein heikles Thema geht. *„To kick the bucket"* ist humorvoll, aber ziemlich respektlos und gehört deshalb nicht in eine Beileidskarte oder Todesanzeige. Ein respektvollerer Euphemismus für *„to die"* ist *„to pass away"*.

to be on somebody's doorstep
wörtlich: auf jemandes Türstufe sein
idiomatisch: vor jemandes Haustür sein

Julia's never been to the museum even though it's right on her doorstep.

to pour money down the drain
wörtlich: Geld den Abfluss hinunterschütten
idiomatisch: das Geld zum Fenster hinauswerfen

The company doesn't need to hire another consultant. It's just pouring money down the drain.

to go back to the drawing board
wörtlich: zum Reißbrett zurückgehen
idiomatisch: noch einmal von vorn anfangen

The council won't give us permission to hold the concert, so we'll have to go back to the drawing board.

to sit on the fence
wörtlich: auf dem Zaun sitzen
idiomatisch: sich neutral verhalten; sich nicht festlegen
  (auch: zwischen zwei Stühlen sitzen)

My brother is constantly trying to get our mum to take his side in an argument, but she always sits on the fence.

 to wipe the floor with somebody

wörtlich: mit jemandem den Boden wischen

idiomatisch: jemanden fertigmachen;
  mit jemandem Schlitten fahren

The Jamaican athlete wiped the floor with the rest of the competitors.

to hold the fort

wörtlich: die Festung halten

idiomatisch: die Stellung halten

Chris needed to go and pick up his grandma from the airport, so Liz agreed to hold the fort at the café while he was gone.

Alles klar?

Jake's Team hat das Spiel leicht gewonnen.
Wie drückt er sich aus?

a) *We cleaned the walls with them.*
b) *We wiped the floor with them.*
c) *We polished the furniture with them.*

to lead somebody up the garden path

wörtlich: jemanden den Gartenpfad hinaufführen

idiomatisch: jemanden an der Nase herumführen;
jemanden hinters Licht führen

The mayor has been leading the residents of the city up the garden path about his political reforms.

to go at it hammer and tongs

wörtlich: es Hammer und Zange anpacken

idiomatisch: sich ins Zeug legen

The deadline is on Friday. We'll have to go at it hammer and tongs this week if we're going to meet it.

to get on like a house on fire

wörtlich: wie ein brennendes Haus miteinander auskommen

idiomatisch: prächtig miteinander auskommen;
sich mit jemandem blendend verstehen

Gareth wasn't sure about his new colleague at first, but now they get on like a house on fire.

to be a household name

wörtlich: ein Haushaltsname sein

idiomatisch: ein Begriff sein; ein vertrauter Name sein

*You haven't heard of Andy Stewart?
He's a household name in Scotland.*

to hit the nail on the head

wörtlich: den Nagel auf den Kopf treffen

idiomatisch: den Nagel auf den Kopf treffen

The president hit the nail on the head when he said
that people were tired of political scandal.

to be a flash in the pan

wörtlich: ein Aufblitzen in der Pfanne sein

idiomatisch: ein Strohfeuer sein; eine Eintagsfliege sein

Everyone is trying to get hold of one of these new gadgets,
but will they just turn out to be a flash in the pan?

– to go at it hammer and tongs –

it's the pot calling the kettle black

wörtlich: es ist der Topf, der den Wasserkessel
  schwarz schimpft

idiomatisch: ein Esel schimpft den anderen Langohr

*The government are saying that the local council
is corrupt? It's the pot calling the kettle black.*

to hit the roof

wörtlich: das Dach treffen

idiomatisch: an die Decke gehen

*Shona's dad hit the roof when he found out
she was pregnant.*

to pull the rug out from under somebody's feet

wörtlich: jdm. den Teppich von unter den Füßen herausziehen

idiomatisch: jdm. den Boden unter den Füßen wegziehen

*Robert's business partner has decided to retire suddenly
and it's really pulled the rug out from under his feet.*

to have a screw loose

wörtlich: eine Schraube locker haben

idiomatisch: eine Schraube locker haben,
  nicht alle Tassen im Schrank haben

*Anyone who wants to go cycling in this weather
must have a screw loose.*

to have a memory like a sieve

wörtlich: ein Gedächtnis wie ein Sieb haben

idiomatisch: ein Gedächtnis wie ein Sieb haben

I'm sorry. I have a memory like a sieve.
What was your name again?

to take everything but the kitchen sink

wörtlich: alles außer der Spüle mitnehmen

idiomatisch: den halben Hausrat mitnehmen

The family were only going away for a fortnight, but
Mum insisted on taking everything but the kitchen sink.

Vorsicht, Ratte!

Das deutsche Wort „*Rat*" sollte man immer ganz vorsichtig
ins Englische übersetzen, denn sein englischer Zwilling „*rat*"
bedeutet „*Ratte*". Die deutsche Redewendung „*den halben
Hausrat mitnehmen*" mit „*to take half the house rat*" zu
übersetzen, löst bestimmt Bestürzung und sogar Ekel unter
Englischsprechenden aus.

to throw a spanner in the works

wörtlich: einen Schraubenschlüssel ins Getriebe werfen

idiomatisch: Sand ins Getriebe streuen;
  jemandes Pläne durchkreuzen

The bank has refused to finance the project,
which has thrown a spanner in the works.

not to be the sharpest tool in the box

wörtlich: nicht das schärfste Werkzeug im Kasten sein

idiomatisch: nicht der / die Klügste / Hellste sein

We can't have Simon on our team for the pub quiz.
He's not exactly the sharpest tool in the box.

to be banging your head against a brick wall

wörtlich: deinen Kopf gegen eine Backsteinmauer schlagen

idiomatisch: mit dem Kopf gegen die Wand rennen;
  auf Granit beißen

I've tried to persuade my daughter not to marry him,
but I feel like I'm banging my head against a brick wall.

to drive somebody up the wall

wörtlich: jemanden die Mauer hinauftreiben

idiomatisch: jemanden auf die Palme bringen;
  jemandem auf den Wecker gehen

Jennifer's noisy neighbours were driving her up the wall,
so she decided to go round and complain.

Alles verstanden?

Welche Redewendung passt zu welcher deutschen Entsprechung? Tragen Sie den Buchstaben der passenden Übersetzung in das Kästchen ein.

1. ☐ *to run like clockwork*
2. ☐ *to hit the roof*
3. ☐ *to drive somebody up the wall*
4. ☐ *to be a flash in the pan*
5. ☐ *to take everything but the kitchen sink*
6. ☐ *not to be the sharpest tool in the box*
7. ☐ *to kick the bucket*
8. ☐ *to have skeletons in the closet*
9. ☐ *to be water under the bridge*
10. ☐ *to lead somebody up the garden path*

a. jemanden auf die Palme bringen **b.** Schnee von gestern sein **c.** den halben Hausrat mitnehmen **d.** den Löffel abgeben **e.** jemanden an der Nase herumführen **f.** an die Decke gehen **g.** nicht der / die Klügste sein **h.** Leichen im Keller haben **i.** ein Strohfeuer sein **j.** wie am Schnürchen laufen

Register Englisch

Alle Redewendungen sind alphabetisch nach dem Hauptstichwort des jeweiligen Ausdrucks sortiert.

Register Deutsch

Alle Redewendungen sind alphabetisch nach dem Hauptstichwort des jeweiligen Ausdrucks sortiert.

Lösungen

Kapitel 1: Tierisch gut!
Quiz: c
Zuordnungsseite: 1 d, 2 g, 3 h, 4 j, 5 f, 6 b, 7 i, 8 c, 9 a, 10 e

Kapitel 2: Gefundenes Fressen
Quiz: c
Zuordnungsseite: 1 j, 2 d, 3 f, 4 c, 5 i, 6 h, 7 b, 8 g, 9 a, 10 e

Kapitel 3: Reine Kopfsache
Quiz: b
Zuordnungsseite: 1 g, 2 a, 3 j, 4 f, 5 i, 6 c, 7 b, 8 e, 9 h, 10 d

Kapitel 4: Am eigenen Leib
Quiz: a
Zuordnungsseite: 1 g, 2 i, 3 e, 4 f, 5 a, 6 b, 7 h, 8 j, 9 c, 10 d

Kapitel 5: In der Natur der Sache
Quiz: c
Zuordnungsseite: 1 g, 2 d, 3 i, 4 j, 5 c, 6 b, 7 e, 8 a, 9 h, 10 f

Kapitel 6: Lifestyler
Quiz: a
Zuordnungsseite: 1 j, 2 h, 3 c, 4 g, 5 d, 6 f, 7 i, 8 a, 9 e, 10 b

Kapitel 7: Farbe bekennen
Quiz: a
Zuordnungsseite: 1 b, 2 d, 3 h, 4 a, 5 g, 6 c, 7 e, 8 i, 9 j, 10 f

Kapitel 8: Zahltag!
Quiz: b
Zuordnungsseite: 1 f, 2 d, 3 j, 4 c, 5 a, 6 h, 7 b, 8 i, 9 e, 10 g

Kapitel 9: Traum vom Eigenheim
Quiz: b
Zuordnungsseite: 1 j, 2 f, 3 a, 4 i, 5 c, 6 g, 7 d, 8 h, 9 b, 10 e